Perspectives

What Makes a Leader?
What Are the Issues?

Flying Start
to Literacy®

Contents

Introduction

Who is a leader you respect and admire?

When people talk about leaders, they are often referring to people who have positions of power and responsibility. They frequently make judgements about national leaders – presidents, prime ministers – who are elected to lead countries. These leaders are famous, and they are judged on the decisions they make.

But there are other people who are not famous that make good things happen, solve problems and influence groups of people. They may be quite young. They may be among your friends.

Do you know someone who is a leader? What qualities do they have that makes them a leader?

VOTES for WOMEN

VOTES
FOR
WOMEN

Girls
are
Great!

Greta Thunberg: Climate change activist

On 20 September 2019, four million people from 161 countries took part in a strike to highlight the climate change crisis and to demand action. The inspiration for this worldwide protest was a Swedish teen, Greta Thunberg, writes Kerrie Shanahan.

How did she do this? How did Greta motivate millions of people from all around the world to join her in fighting for change?

Who is Greta Thunberg?

Greta was born in 2003, and at the age of eight, she became aware of climate change and the issues surrounding it. She was alarmed that this huge problem was not being addressed by many world leaders and decided to learn all that she could about the dire situation.

In May 2018, at the age of 15, Greta won a writing competition about climate change. This sparked the beginning of her crusade to make people aware of the urgency of the crisis.

Later that year, Greta decided to take action. Instead of going to school, she sat by herself outside the Swedish parliament to protest. Greta held her "school strike for climate" every day for three weeks. Other students heard about Greta's protest and started to join her strike.

News spread about Greta's campaign, and students in other parts of the world were inspired to hold "school strike for climate" protests in their communities. As time went on, the movement evolved into a worldwide weekly protest. Somewhere in the world, students strike each week to address global climate issues.

Greta received more and more publicity because of the climate protests, and as a result, she got to speak to many world leaders.

Greta Thunberg meets with world leaders at the 2019 European Economic and Social Committee event held in Davos, Switzerland.

UN Climate Action Summit 2019

On 23 September 2019, Greta was invited to give a speech at the United Nations (UN) climate action summit, in New York, in the United States. Her words made news around the world.

Greta is not a president or a prime minister. She's not a princess or the CEO (chief executive officer) of a company. But she is one of the most influential leaders in our world today when it comes to climate change.

Many people admire Greta, but she does face opposition. Some politicians say she is too young and too naive to know what she is talking about, but Greta disagrees, explaining:

"Being young is a great advantage, since we see the world from a new perspective and we are not afraid to make radical changes."

Greta has become a role model and an inspiration, and she is proof that, as she says, you're "never too small to make a difference".

Here is some of Greta's speech at the UN Climate Action Summit, which was held in New York City on 23 September 2019.

This is all wrong. I shouldn't be up here. I should be back in school on the other side of the ocean. Yet you all come to us young people for hope. How dare you!

You have stolen my dreams and my childhood with your empty words. And yet I'm one of the lucky ones. People are suffering. People are dying. Entire ecosystems are collapsing. We are in the beginning of a mass extinction, and all you can talk about is money and fairy tales of eternal economic growth. How dare you!

For more than 30 years, the science has been crystal clear. How dare you continue to look away and come here saying that you're doing enough, when the politics and solutions needed are still nowhere in sight.

How dare you pretend that this can be solved with just "business as usual" and some technical solutions? With today's emissions levels, that remaining CO_2 budget will be entirely gone within less than 8 $^1/_2$ years.

We will not let you get away with this. Right here, right now is where we draw the line. The world is waking up. And change is coming, whether you like it or not.

Thank you.

Should we listen to young people?

Teenager Ruth Quinn has attended a number of climate action marches over the past couple of years. In this article, Ruth writes about how young leaders such as Greta Thunberg inspire her.

Do you agree with Ruth? Why do you think we should listen to young people?

People under the age of 18 make up almost 30 per cent of the world's population, yet we are often overlooked when it comes to making decisions that predominantly affect us. And climate change, in the opinion of many people, including me, is the biggest challenge in our world.

If we are the generation growing up into this world, why don't we get some say in what happens to it? Although we may not be able to dictate the actions of world leaders or the CEO of a big coal company, or even vote yet, it is important that we don't become discouraged by the idea that we can't do anything. Everyone has a voice – but how you choose to use it is what really matters.

In August 2018, Greta Thunberg decided she had a voice and with it, she could make a difference. Since then, she has become a great force for change in the world. On 20 September 2019, millions of people all over the world (including myself) joined her in a global "strike for climate" protest march.

I think that Greta is an amazing advocate for climate action, and what she has done is inspiring, eye-opening and crucial. She has shown us that when we all come together, our voices aren't just small whispers but a strong, united and unavoidable roar.

I have been going to these school strikes for climate for almost a year and a half, and I do this because I can't stand by and do nothing – climate action is something I am passionate about. To me, this isn't negotiable – it's our future and I care about it. In 40 years, I don't want to be in a polluted world ruined by greed, and with millions of animals extinct.

I am part of a global movement. My generation is fighting for change, and being a part of it is confronting, but the fire of unison is not going to be put out anytime soon. In the words of Thunberg: "Change is coming, whether you like it or not."

The people in power can no longer pretend they have everything under control. They can no longer look down on us because we are "too young" and "shouldn't be ditching school for no reason".

In reality, taking part in the climate movement is hardly a choice; this is bigger than missing one maths lesson. This is my life, my future, my children's future and it's time we started to act like it.

Speak out!

Read what these students think about the qualities that make a good leader.

What perspectives do you agree with? What other ideas do you have?

A good leader needs to be able to communicate well so that everyone knows exactly what they believe in. Even if a leader has good communication skills, they must realise that not everyone will agree with them. They might face opposition, and so they need to have a "thick skin" when things don't go right, or when people criticise them.

Leaders can't always be perfect. Sometimes, they will make mistakes. A good leader needs to take responsibility when things go wrong and face up to their mistakes. But then they need to put that behind them and keep on going. They need to be positive, resilient and really confident.

A good leader must put on a positive face for the people who believe in them. This is especially important if there is a crisis. Leaders must not panic in an emergency or if something goes wrong. They need to be calm and give confidence to the people who believe in them, and in what they are doing.

A good leader must be passionate about their beliefs and know what they want to get done. If they are passionate and believe in their actions, then other people will follow their lead.

Thai cave rescue

In June 2018, a dozen members of the Thai Wild Boar youth soccer team and their assistant coach decided to venture into a cave system in Thailand known as Tham Luang.

When the caves started to fill with water, writes Joshua Hatch, the coach led the team deeper into the cave system, where they became stranded. How did the coach turn the life-threatening situation around? What qualities of a leader did he show?

The Tham Luang cave system runs under a mountain range for more than 10 kilometres, and it is a popular place for locals and tourists to visit. But, it's also a dangerous place. During the rainy season between May and October, rains can quickly flood the caves with five metres of water.

And it was during the rainy season that the 12 boys and their coach, Ekkapol "Ake" Chantawong, entered the caves on 23 June 2018.

The boys ranged in age from 11 to 17. The coach wasn't much older – just 25. They had no reason to think anything would go wrong when they entered the first cave. And if they had stayed near the first cave's entrance, they would have been fine. But, they decided to go deeper into the cave than they should have. And then, without warning, water from recent rains began to flood their passage. The boys and Coach Ake were stuck.

To escape the rising waters, Coach Ake and the boys moved to higher ground as quickly as they could. Unfortunately, that meant going deeper into the cave and further from the entrance. Worst of all, nobody knew they were there.

Thai cave rescue

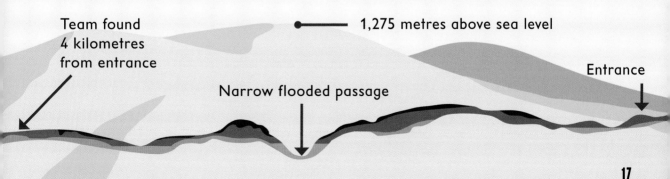

Team found
4 kilometres
from entrance

1,275 metres above sea level

Entrance

Narrow flooded passage

Soon, the boys' parents started looking for them. They discovered the boys' bikes at the caves' entrance and figured out what happened. Then the Thai government started to work out a rescue plan.

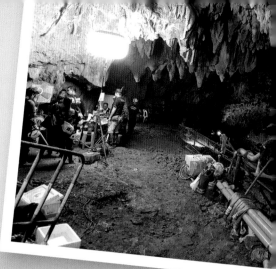

Rescue divers set up their equipment inside the caves.

Coach Ake and the boys were stranded four to five kilometres from the entrance. They had no food or water, no way to communicate to the outside world and only a couple of torches. The cave was cold and dark. They had no idea if anyone would come to their rescue. Coach Ake had gotten the boys into this mess. And it was his responsibility to keep them alive. He started by teaching the boys meditation. This helped the boys remain calm, conserve air and preserve their strength. He showed them how to get drips of fresh water from the cave walls. He also demonstrated how to huddle to keep warm.

Outside the caves, hundreds of people gathered to help with the search. A week after the boys disappeared, specially trained divers managed to swim through the flooded cavern until they reached the boys. All 12 of them and Coach Ake were alive. The Wild Boars had been found, but they weren't yet rescued. The divers brought food and water to the boys, and stayed with them in the dark, wet cave.

Meanwhile, others strategised how to get them out. Day after day, rescuers tried to come up with a plan. Weather forecasters predicted more rain, which would further flood the caves. Oxygen in the cave was running low. Time was running out.

Divers strapped each boy inside a stretcher with an oxygen tank. The divers followed the guide rope to exit the cave system.

On 7 July, more than two weeks after the boys entered the first cave, the rescuers decided it was time to act.

Divers lightly sedated the boys and Coach Ake, and attached oxygen masks and tanks to them. They were then pulled through the dark, cold waters. The rescue operation took three days. Once they were extracted from the cave system, the boys and Coach Ake were taken to a hospital for treatment for pneumonia and other infections. They all made full recoveries.

In the end, all the Wild Boars were rescued, though one diver died. But for 18 days, Coach Ake was able to keep all the boys on his team calm and alive. He may have made a poor decision that got them into trouble in the first place, but his leadership kept them alive so they could be rescued. It just goes to show that most leaders can make mistakes, but in the end, great leaders rise to the occasion, like Coach Ake did.

What type of leader is best?

What type of leader is best? asks writer Kerrie Shanahan. There is no simple answer to this question. Leaders have a range of skills and qualities, and different situations call for different leadership styles.

As you read the following scenarios, think about the qualities that a leader would need to solve the specific problem, to get things done, to stand up for what is fair or to get out of a sticky situation!

What leadership quality is most needed in each instance?

Project panic!

Your teacher has created random groups of five students to complete a project about endangered animals. You love this topic, but your group is a disaster! One person keeps mucking up. Two others are continuously chatting and giggling. The other member of your group has lots of ideas, but you don't see the merit in any of them. *My ideas are much better,* you think.

"Make sure you work as a group," your teacher says. That's helpful! Time is ticking away and we must finish at lunchtime. You start to panic . . .

Which leadership style would best help solve this problem? Who would be best to get the group on track?

Ollie open-minded	Ella the enthusiastic one	Willow the worker
Ollie listens to everyone's ideas and tries to see all points of view. He doesn't judge, and is willing to try a new approach or solution.	Ella is a glass-half-full person. She is positive and passionate about her beliefs, and her enthusiasm is infectious.	Willow gets things done! She's organised, efficient and persistent. She works hard and keeps trying, no matter how tough things get.

The big splash

You and your friends love going to the swimming pool, but one day, things go wrong! Right in front of the No Diving sign, one of your friends jumps up high and makes a huge splash. Water goes everywhere. Your friends all roar with laughter. You join in, too, even though you don't think the situation is funny. Suddenly, the lifeguard arrives.

"Not funny!" he bellows. "Who was it?" Silence. Not one of your friends speaks. "If you don't tell me who did this," the lifeguard continues, "you're all banned!"

You swallow hard. You don't want to be banned. That's not fair! But no one is saying a word.

What leadership quality do you most need? Who could probably help you solve this problem?

Ryan responsible	Claire creative	Sophia the speaker
Ryan does the right thing. He follows the rules and he reminds others what the rules are, too.	Claire is a good problem solver. She comes up with the craziest ideas, but sometimes that's just what's needed!	Sophia can talk her way out of anything. She's good at persuading others to see her point of view.

Problems at the park

You're excited. It's the first time your mum has allowed you to walk to the park without her. Your big brother said he'll be there to look after you. When you arrive at the park, your big brother's friends are there. They want to go to an area that has been marked off with barrier tape and your brother agrees.

"We're not allowed in there," you tell your brother. "Look at the signs. The tracks are dangerous and they're being fixed."

Your brother says not to worry – your parents won't know if you go. It doesn't feel right, but you follow your brother and his friends past the tape. About half an hour later, your brother trips on a loose slat in the boardwalk. "Owwww," he groans. "My ankle!" Everyone freezes. What will you do now?

What sort of leadership qualities would you need here? Who would be best to solve this problem? Why?

Dakota the decision maker	Kyle the kind one	Theo the thinker
If you need someone to make a hard decision, it's Dakota! She's confident and cool in a crisis.	Kyle has a big heart! He relies on his emotions to guide him. He has empathy and is always ready to help others.	Theo thinks about the problem and sums up everything. He asks good questions. He's the "brains" of the group.

What is your opinion? How to write a persuasive argument

1. State your opinion

Think about the issues related to your topic. What is your opinion?

2. Research

Research the information you need to support your opinion.

Related *Perspectives* book   Internet   Other sources

3. Make a plan

Introduction
How will you "hook" the reader?
State your opinion.

List reasons to support your opinion.
What persuasive devices will you use?

Reason 1
Support your reason
with evidence and details.

Reason 2
Support your reason
with evidence and details.

Reason 3
Support your reason
with evidence and details.

Conclusion
Restate your opinion. Leave your reader with a strong message.

4. Publish

Publish your persuasive argument.
Use visuals to reinforce your opinion.